In the name of God

***

Unwithering Flames: Book-3 "Shaheed Afifeh; Narrated by His Wife" by: Alemeh Tahmasbi
Copyright © 2023 Green Palm

All rights reserved. No portion of this book may be reproduced in any form without permission from the publisher. For permissions contact: info@greenpalm.net
Translated and edited by: Green Palm books
Cover by Hussein Reza Vanaki
First Edition

To contribute in the publishing process and be informed about other volumes of the series, please contact info@greenpalm.net

Unwithering Flames

──────── Book 3 - Afifeh ────────

In order to have a fruitful and prosperous relationship, people have come to terms that they must love one another. Unfortunately, the meaning of true love has been lost. Many have relegated love to just intimacy between a man and a woman. However, this is just the initial stage of true love, and we must aspire to reach a higher level beyond mere physical attraction. Such love is built on the foundation of honesty, enjoyment, selflessness, and spiritual attainment. Although many strive to reach this transcendent form of love, the affairs of this world become a barrier for them.

This series of books entitled *Unwithering Flames* recounts to us stories of those men and women who in the events of the Islamic Revolution and the Iraq's war against Iran turned away from this world just for the sake of God. In doing so, they became lovers in the true sense. They had the type of love that did not just make the pain of this world bearable, rather it was something beautiful for them. The love whose flame has not dimmed even with martyrdom or death.

🌐 www.GREENPALM.net
✈ 📞 +98 999 99 16 140
✉ info@GREENPALM.net

Shaban Ali Afifeh

Birth: June 13, 1958
Marriage to Tooba Mo'tamed: August 28, 1984
Martyrdom: April 7, 1987

SYNOPSIS

When the years of youth passes away, you reach middle age and return to the days when you had just started your married life; you observe how beautifully God has arranged all events for you so that your body and soul would be bound to someone whose companionship requires merit.

Joining Ali was not easy; it had its price, a hefty price that Tooba was ready to pay to make Ali the first and last love of her life—a love that is still alive and enduring, and even more, Tooba feels its sweetness each day.

Contents

Chapter 1
An Unsteady Decision..9

Chapter 2
The Unforeseen Proposal..31

Chapter 3
A Difficult Promise..55

Chapter 4
Hand in a Prosthetic Hand at Our Wedding......71

Chapter 5
The Official Officer..91

Chapter 6
Take Me to Lady Zahra (s) on Your Wings........101

Chapter 1

An Unsteady Decision

She was standing adamant on attending hawza[1]. Her parents did not disagree; however, they did say, "You can attend hawza after finishing high school." The more they tried, the less she conceded. She had given up school and remained home, constantly emphasizing, "I have to go study the books of our religion." Observing her stubbornness, her mother resorted to the principals and teachers. However, she had made up her mind. She was determined to go to hawza, whatever

---

1. The Islamic seminary (*ḥawza ʿilmiyya*) is a religious educational institute, where its graduates are known as clerics.

> *it took. Her father knew she was too young to go there, and it would not end well. He made his final say.*
>
> *"No!"*
>
> *Seeing her father's inflexibility, she sought solutions. Although it was the first time she had insisted so much, she threw caution to the wind. She was not present at the dining table. She even abstained from food when they brought the meal to her room. Seeing her mother giving her angry looks or raising her voice at her, she ate only one date. She starved herself so much that her father could no longer tolerate it and let her go.*

Our house was in the new city of Lar, in the south of Fars province. The story behind the new Lar and old Lar dates back to many years ago, i.e., 1960. At the time, when my father and mother were newly married, the city was destroyed, and the buildings collapsed in a severe earthquake. Many people died under the rubble. Our small city was utterly destroyed. So, they did not rebuild it anew, rather they began to construct buildings a few kilometers away. Each family was given about 400-500 square meters of land. There are no alleys in the new Lar, only streets. Later on, when some people revived the earthquake-stricken part of the city, Lar was divided into the old and new city. Our home was also located in one of the streets of the new Lar.

There were two nested rooms on one side and a small kitchen on the other. Our house's *howz*[2] was also in the middle of the yard. Alongside the *howz*, there was a ziziphus tree and we rested under its shade during the summers. Walking through the bitter orange and palm trees, we reached the other side of the yard, where the washbasin, bathroom, and cellar were located. My dad had dug a few meters into the ground and constructed an underground room, which we called the cellar. Many people had constructed such a room at the other end of their yard. It had a domed roof. We had also made a storeroom above the cellar. A few meters away, we kept a number of hens and roosters, to which a sheep was added every year as Eid al-Adha[3] drew near.

---

2. A *howz* is a pool filled with water. It is often built in yards of houses and made from stones, blocks, and cement.

3. One of the official holdiays in the Islamic calender in which Muslims honor Abraham's willingness to sacrifice his son Ishmael (in Bible, it is Isaac) as an act of obedience to God's command.

I was the third child and the second daughter of the family. We were seven children: Ziba, Hamid, Tooba, Zhila, Vida, Vahid, and Saeid. I was the most playful and mischievous among the children. I was very fearless. Sometimes, we were naughty and annoyed *Aghajaan*,⁴ our father, when he was asleep. He would get angry, shout and chase after us. He could never get me, and I was the last one to be caught if ever he could. He was panting when he was able to get his hands on me. Now when I think of it, I feel pity for him. However, the mischievous behavior soon ended.

I went to school both in the mornings and evenings. I came home at noon, had lunch quickly, completed my prayers, and went to school again. When I was a fourth-grade student, I wore my floral *chador*⁵ and went to the mosque during the holidays to attend the Quran-teaching classes of

---

4. *Aghajaan* is a nickname for fathers and grandfathers nationwide in Iran.

5. A *chador* is a long cloak-like garment, which covers the entire body, worn by Muslim women in Iran and some other countries in public places. The official *chador* is typically black. For prayer, however, a white *chador* is worn and in certain gatherings colorful chadors are used.

Mr. Noorbakhsh. At home, my father encouraged us to memorize short *surahs*.⁶ He smiled and gave us one toman for each surah memorized or every top score we received at school. However, for memorizing *Āyatul-Kursī*⁷ (the Throne verse), he rewarded us with ten tomans.⁸ I collected all the money he gifted me to buy books. I was never tired of reading. I loved storybooks.

The books written by Mahmood Hakimi and many other authors were my kind friends during those days. I was always willing to sacrifice my sleep to read books. At midnight, when everyone was sound asleep, I used to sneak into the bathroom to read books in order not to wake *Aghajaan*, as he was very sensitive to light when sleeping.

My father worked for the municipality. Every morning, he donned his coat, fastened

---

6. Surah is the equivalent of chapter in the Quran.
7. *Ayat al-Kursi* or Verse of *al-Kursi* is a Quranic verse, the recitation of which is rewarding in the hereafter. Muslims recite it for protection against catastrophes and unexpected incidents. It is verse 255 of *Surah al-Baqara*. It is often recited along with its following two verses.
8. The Iranian currency.

his tie, and went to the office. He was very disciplined and well-organized throughout, from doing daily chores to grocery shopping. He did all the shopping, even our shoes and clothes. He was a big spender when it came to buying things for his children. If we wanted something, he went and bought not one, but many of them. We were well-off economically. Most people ate rice only once a week, but we had rice every day. We felt no deficiencies or inadequacies. Apart from *Aghajaan*'s impeccable planning, the endeavors of my mother cannot easily be forgotten. She was an all-rounder—weaving, sewing, cookery, and calligraphy. I never fail to remember her culinary skills when preparing *Sholezard*[9] and *Aash*.[10] She never turned a blind eye to raising her children properly, either. For example, not one of the children would touch the food despite being hungry until *Aghajaan* came

---

9. *Sholezard* is a traditional Iranian dessert, made from rice, sugar, cardamom, and rose water. It is yellow because of the addition of saffron. Iranians often distribute *sholezard* as a religious vow on religious occasions.

10. *Aash* is an Iranian dish made out of vegetables and thick noodles.

to sit at the table. There was no force; we could not find it in our hearts to start eating. My mother had raised us in such a way. She wanted us to respect *Aghajaan*.

Our house was always crowded. Our relatives were constantly coming and going—mostly my aunts. My mother prepared a kind of food specific to the Lar region, called *La'ie*. She stewed chickpeas and potatoes along with a lot of meat in rice. We would spread a large tablecloth when my aunts came, and we all sat around it. We loved our aunts very much. We would have liked them to stay longer when they came. They were like sisters to my mom and adored by all of us. Sometimes, when *Aghajaan*'s mother came to our home, we had her stay with us for one or two years. My mother had lost her parents during childhood and loved my grandmother like her own mother. She looked out for my father's mother when she came. She took my grandmother to the doctor as soon as she felt a bit unwell. I always slept on the same pillow with my grandmother in order to wake up if she ever moved, so that I could give her anything she wanted, just in case. She prayed for our happiness and blessing a lot in her midnight prayers.

For me, it was important to take advantage of opportunities in a proper manner and learn new things every day. Every year, when the academic season finished, we went to the library at the Center for the Intellectual Development of Children and Adolescents (CIDCA) with our friends. We also went there during the winter sometimes, but we were hardly at home during the summer. The trainers at CIDCA either read us books or performed plays. It was a long way to the library, but we never felt tired. It was so exciting and motivating for us to go there, that we were able to endure the long distance. Apart from the CIDCA, I also had a membership at the small library near our home in order to borrow books.

During the time of the revolutionary struggle, I became more inclined to read books about revolution and ethics, mostly the works of Ayatollah Dastgheib[11] and

---

11. Ayatollah Seyyed Abdol Hussein Dastgheib Shirazi (1913-1981) was a religious scholar in Iran, a member of the Assembly of Experts for the Constitution, Imam Khomeini's representative in Fars Province, and the Imam of Friday Prayer in Shiraz. He was assassinated and martyred by forces of People's Mojahedin Organization (MEK or Rajavi's sect) in 1981, when he was on his way for Friday Prayer.

Shaheed *Motahhari*.[12] Those days, we were so energetic and always busy. *Aghajaan* had just bought a car. He picked us up and took us to a revolutionary demonstration or a funeral ceremony of the martyrs. After all, he bought the car intending to take us to the demonstrations. In the morning, we went to the demonstrations in the old Lar and spent evenings in the new Lar. One day, when my grandmother had stayed in our home and my mother was going to take her to the doctor, the rest of us went to the demonstrations. We even took Saeid with us, despite the fact that he was only an infant. The guards were shooting heavily and had opened fire on the demonstrators. I was running around with Saeid in my arms. Looking at me, people said, "Go home! Why have you brought the baby here? It's dangerous!" I told them, "It would be a moment of immense pride for us if our baby is martyred in the path of Imam Khomeini and the Revolution."

---

12. Ayatollah Shaheed Morteza Motahhari (1919-1979) was an Iranian author, a seminary and university professor of Islamic philosophy and theology in Iran, Four months into the Islamic Revolution, however, he was assassinated and martyred at the hands of the terrorist group, Forqan. In Iran, the anniversary of his martyrdom (Ordibehesht 12th / May 2nd) is named as Teacher's Day.

Aghajaan had already retired from the municipality by the time the Revolution materialized, and had opened a shop manufacturing cabinets. He worked there alongside my brother. In the days leading up to Nowruz[13] in the year 1980, my dad bought clothes for all of us. I loved my shirt. It was purple with golden brocades hanging from it. I wished Nowruz would come sooner so that I could wear my shirt to the parties hosted by our relatives. That never happened, though. I was a first-grade high school student. They held a celebration in the school. "Everyone can bring anything they want in order to donate to those who are less advantaged," they said. I became heavy-hearted and grief-stricken when I heard those words from my teacher. After getting permission from my mother, I gift-wrapped my new shirt and took it to school. It was very hard for me to loosen my hold on it, but I tried to get over it and give it away. At the time, our actions were influenced by the mood set by the Revolution. When

---

13. Nowruz is the Persian-language term for the first day of the Iranian New Year. It begins on the spring and marks the beginning of Farvardin, the first month of the Solar Hijri calendar.

the Revolution became victorious, we were so excited that we would help in any possible way. We were working on our beliefs too. Various types of classes were held in Imam Jafar Sadiq (a) Mosque in our neighborhood. I remember that I enrolled in the worldview and self-awareness classes with my friends. When I heard that Imam Khomeini fasted on Mondays and Thursdays, I decided to do the same. Up to four years, I ate light meals for *iftar*,[14] such as bread and dates. But at the time of *suhoor*,[15] if I did not eat rice, my mother would frown, "You will become feeble, girl!" she said. She simmered with anger when I managed to inflict such hardships on myself. She contacted my principal at school and asked them to force me to eat something. She was right, however. I was really going to extremes with it all. Even on days when I was not fasting, I only ate a piece of bread and a few dates. I really loved to suffer from hunger. Simultaneously, I was so

---

14. A meal taken by Muslims at sunset to break fasting.
15. *Suhoor* or also called *sahari* or *sahūr*, is the meal consumed early in the morning by Muslims before fasting.

busy with my classes and Basij[16] affairs that I was totally inundated. After the Revolution settled, there were large demonstrations still taking place. We managed to think up some slogans for these demonstrations, then wrote them on cardboard and gave them out to people. I loved to do whatever I could for the Revolution. I even chose the vocational training discipline to learn typewriting, which was very useful in Basij-related activities. We were constantly busy typing material and pasting them on the walls. During the holidays, I was busy doing these types of things the entire day. *Aghajaan* always said, "Tooba, we should probably bring your pillow and blanket over to the mosque."

Attending too many classes had made a teacher out of me. I felt like I had to teach what I had learned to the younger kids. I held Quran classes in one of the rooms of our house. The children in our neighborhood and those of our relatives and

---

16. The Basij Resistance Force is a volunteer paramilitary organization operating under the Islamic Revolutionary Guards Corps (IRGC). After the Iraq war against Iran, this force still plays a role in various fields in which widespread participation of people or public services are required.

friends attended them. Our school deputy, Mrs. Eftekhar, also brought her child. When she found out how many books I had and how enthusiastic I was about reading, she appointed me as the school librarian. She handed me the keys and said, "You know how you should take it forward." I opened the door, went in, and started to tidy it up. I piled up the photos of the Shah and threw them away. While cleaning out the closets, I came up with a number of photos peeking out of the album. I grabbed one of them. My heart suddenly sank, and I burst into tears. In the picture, some of the children from our school were at a party with the SAVAK[17] officials. I became high-strung. I did not know what to do. I went to the principal's office and privately told her the story. She wanted me to tear them up and throw them away. I shredded them, threw them into a black plastic bag, and put it in the trash bin.

---

17. Intelligence and Security Organization of Country, abbreviated in Persian as SAVAK, was the security institute of the Pahlavi regime, which was founded in 1957 under the support and planning of the US, to enhance the monitoring of political dissidents and with the motto of "protecting the safety of the country."

The library could not be cleaned and sorted out in one or two days. Every day, when I had finished my classes, I was granted permission from my teacher and went to the library. At break times, and even when the school bell rang, I stayed in the library. I worked until the janitor finished his work. I numbered and tagged the books. Finally, I arranged the library as I liked, and it became tidy and organized. It was so well-sorted that I could pick the books my teacher asked for, blindfolded from a particular closet, shelf, and number. Part of the library had been assigned to cassette tape collections. IRGC[18] and Basij gave us cassettes, and we would loan them out to the school girls. The cassettes contained Imam Khomeini's orations and speeches as well as those of other scholars. I also took the cassettes home to listen to. Sometimes, I wrote some of their sentences on the

---

18. Islamic Revolutionary Guard Corps, or *Sepah*, is a military and cultural organization, which was established about three months after the victory of the Islamic Revolution of Iran (in April 1979) under Imam Khomeini's advisement to protect the revolution and its achievements and to cooperate with the army of the Islamic Republic of Iran.

cardboards and pasted them on the wall. This was our state of affairs when the war broke out. It was during this time that I was literally hard at work. Every day after school, I went to the Basij base. During the evenings, I was busy weaving crochet hats for combatants on the frontlines. I had not one but numerous preoccupations. In the library, I did things stealthily. For example, I would put articles related to the Islamic Republican Party and Mr. Beheshti[19] inside the books. When it was traced back to me, I would say, "I only loaned the books in here; how can you know it was me?!" I played my role well. No one believed it could be me. The only one who knew everything was my friend. She took the papers from her brother-in-law, who worked for the IRGC. I felt heavy-hearted and sad from the unfounded and unsubstantiated accusations they made up against Mr. Beheshti. I didn't want other girls to be misled about it.

In the final academic year of high school, the school buzzed with rumors that

---

19. Ayatollah Shaheed Sayyid Muhammad Husseini Beheshti (1928-1981) was one of the greatest students of Imam Khomeini and a modern scholar in the religious context of Iran.

a presenter was to come and give a speech. A few female seminary scholars came from Fasa[20] and told us about its atmosphere. Their words appealed to me. I thought, "I have to go, whatever it takes." And just like that, the idea came to my mind to leave for Fasa. I did everything I could from my side, and eventually, my parents conceded.

In February-March 1984, I packed up my suitcase and, with my friends, we set out on our journey. There were four of us, and I was the youngest. We got on a bus and departed toward Shiraz and then Fasa. It took nine and a half hours to get there. On the way there, I was both restless and excited. I couldn't believe I was going to *hawza*. When we arrived in Fasa, all of the city's boulevards were full of bitter orange and cherry trees. It was such a refreshing sight for us, but people out there were indifferently passing by the trees.

After searching, we reached the Hazrat Fatemeh (s) School. The seminary building

---

20. Fasa is an ancient populated city in the Fars Province, located fifty kilometers in the southeast of Shiraz. Nearly 1100 people from Fasa (and its surrounding area) were martyred in defense of the Islamic Revolution.

was south-facing. There was a very big L-shaped room where our classes were held on the right side. There was also a bedroom next to it. The two rooms were separated by closets, into which the girls put their blankets. There was a short wall between this room and the classroom. Sometimes, when the girls got sick, they stayed in this room to hear the instructor speaking. The office was on the left side, as well as the restroom and bathroom. Besides the office, there was a room belonging to Mr. Zahadat, the son-in-law of Ayatollah Dastgheib. He was our instructor and imam of congregational prayers. On the other side of the building, there was a small yard.

We divided the tasks from the very beginning. In turn, one of the girls cooked food, another did the cleaning, and another girl did other chores. I was very overjoyed. We often had classes. There were fifty or sixty students in the public classes and ten or twelve in the private ones. We had discussions after the classes. When it was my turn, I did my job as quickly as possible to get back to my lessons and homework. I did not eat much and fasted on Mondays and Thursdays, as usual. My goal was to make the most of this place. When the girls gathered together, I was busy with my own studies and rarely joined them. I always said, "This is an opportunity to seize." After busying myself with my studies and books for about a month, Nowruz of 1984 came, and I had to get back home.

The spring altered the atmosphere of our house. We would engage in house cleaning, planting fresh and colorful flowers in the garden, revisiting relatives, etc. Every year, around two or three weeks before Nowruz, the gardener would come to plant various types of flowers in our garden.

When the flowers blossomed, the floral scent of the jasmines and roses was mesmerizing. I would sit on the edge of the garden and picked them one by one. I made bouquets of flowers and put them on the Nowruz's tablecloth. *Aghajaan* read the Quran and gave us *Eidi*[21] from between its pages. We went to visit our relatives. When our get-togethers with relatives would come to an end, within three or four

---

21. *Eidi* is a gift Muslims give to younger people on religious occasions, such as *Eid al-Ghadir*, *Eid al-Fitr*, and *Eid al-Adha*. Iranians commonly give *eidi* for Nowruz (the Iranian New Year) as well.

days to *Sizdah Bedar*,[22] we went into the wilderness. Even when we didn't have a car, we took hold of our backpacks and wended our way into the desert along with my aunts and their children. When we arrived at the desert, we opened up our backpacks and settled on a pleasant corner near the palm trees. We would fasten ropes to the trees and swing. Men also divided themselves into teams and played either football or volleyball. They would also piggyback each other as a penalty for losing in a game. We enjoyed and clapped when my father was going to be piggybacked by others. We had lots of fun. At lunch or dinner, we would spread out a large tablecloth. We managed to clean the dishes by the water in the pond. There were many cisterns in the desert, and sometimes men put buckets in to draw water; we used it to wash the dishes. Also, towards the end of the day, we gathered vegetables from among the greenery and took them home. Spring brought along

---

22. *Sizdah Bedar* (literally, getting rid of the thirteen) is an ancient Iranian tradition, celebrated by Iranians on the thirteenth of *Farvardin* (the first month of the Iranian calendar) when they spend time outside of their homes and surrounded by nature.

heavy, brief showers. Whenever *Aghajaan* heard the pitter-patter sound of the rain on the roof, he would run into the yard and put buckets under the gutters to collect the rainwater. In this way, he irrigated the trees and flowers for days.

I went back to *hawza* when the Nowruz holidays of 1984 came to an end. After Nowruz, I wasn't in the mood to pay close attention to my classes and discussions like before. Every time I started to study, I would remember my parents' faces. I missed my family, friends, Basij, school, and the library. It was too soon for me to come to *hawza*, and above all, I was giving myself a hard time. All of this had made me become weary. In the middle of May, I realized I needed to leave Fasa, I folded my clothes, collected my books, and packed my suitcase. The next day, looking around the room, I thought to myself, "*I'll come back after attaining my diploma.*" On the way back home, I was literally cheerful. After arriving home, my family saw my suitcase and found out I had no plans on going back to *hawza*. They didn't bat an eyelid, though. No one asked me why I returned home or why I left the seminary. It seemed they were thankful for my return. They had expected this day to arrive. When I saw my parents were so delighted, I was even more pleased with myself.

Chapter 2

The Unforeseen Proposal

When deciding to obtain my high school diploma, I knew I had to sit for the final exams held in June. I was away from school for two and a half months, and from math, statistics, and arithmetic, and so, getting back on track with these courses after missing a few months was no easy task. Moreover, I did not have a teacher. I had to self-study. Despite the difficulties, I managed to read the books one by one and tried to gear myself up for the exam. When I took the report card, I couldn't take my eyes off those low grades. I felt miserable and downcast and could not help crying for some days. My mother, *Aghajaan*, Ziba, and Hamid did their best to calm me down, but in vain. I became frustrated when I thought

I couldn't get a diploma and had also left *hawza*. I constantly blamed myself. One night, I pondered a lot and finally made up my mind to start everything anew.

The next morning, I woke up as if I had not been crying my heart out the previous night. I washed my hands and face and sat at the tablecloth with puffy eyes that stood out a mile away, showing clearly that I had been crying profusely. My actions were so strange that my mother always said, "Tooba! I always knew that you were different from your siblings!" I always smiled and was tickled pink when I heard that. Seeing me now, I knew she would repeat those words.

After having breakfast and doing the dishes, I called my friend, Farahnaz. Her husband was a seminary student. Spending a few months in the seminary, I found the Arabic language to my taste. I thought to myself, "I can learn Arabic herein at home, too." I talked to my friend to ask her husband if he could teach me Arabic. Her husband replied, "We can hold classes if there are enough students." I talked to a number of girls from relatives and neighbors. We reached a quorum of six students and initiated the classes.

The first day of class coincided with the first day of the month of Ramadan, and the weather was sweltering, too. We had classes every other day, in the afternoons. Farahnaz's husband, Mr. Khalil Azad, held classes in one of the rooms in their house. My never-ending questions began from the very first day. Mr. Khalil Azad answered all of my questions in sequence. I asked so many questions that he felt the enthusiasm in me and found out how many unanswered inquiries I had. I quickly reviewed the whole lesson when I arrived home and noted my questions. Again, two days later, I started asking questions in class. While other girls had a difficult time due to thirst and physical weakness, I was irresistibly asking questions.

The month of Ramadan that year was very hard. We were getting so tanned by the hot air. When there was a blistering sun in the yard, we resorted to the cellar. It was a little cooler than the room. We had also set up a ceiling fan there, to be used when necessary. Sometimes, my siblings and I would lay down in the cellar lethargically. In the meantime, I kept my books in hand and took a look at them every now and then. When it came to the point that I was unable to bear the heat any further, I would also lay down on the floor, like the others. Around sunset, I climbed up the palm tree and picked dates for *iftar*. At home, the only ones who could climb up the tree were my brothers and I. My sisters couldn't manage it.

We were about halfway through the month of Ramadan. One day after class, Farahnaz came up to me and said, "Mr. Khalil Azad has something to tell you." Surprised, I asked, "Me!?" "Yes," she replied. When everyone left, he approached me and asked some questions regarding the class. "Are you happy with the class?" he asked. I thanked him and said, "Everything is OK." Suddenly, he asked, "Do you know Afifeh, Ms. Mo'tamed?" I looked at Farahnaz and asked, "Is that a girl or a boy?" Both were silent; Mr. Khalil Azad smiled, though. Arriving at home, as soon as I approached Hamid, I asked, "Hamid! Do you know Afifeh?" I didn't know who he or she was. I didn't know he was going to propose to me. I asked this question directly in front of my parents, "I only know that he is a *Maddah*,"[23] Hamid said. It never crossed my

---

23. *Maddah* is a religious eulogist who performs at religious ceremonies or commemoration of martyrs and Shia Imams.

mind that maybe something had happened that Mr. Khalil Azad laughed like that, that day. I was completely oblivious. I thought to myself, "*Now, after realizing my brother knows him, let me tell Farahnaz that he is a Maddah. Maybe Mr. Khalil Azad needs to talk to him.*" I called Farahnaz on the telephone and said, "Hamid says he is a *Maddah*." Farahnaz didn't say anything. She changed the subject, and we said our goodbyes.

A week later, Farahnaz asked me to stay again after the class. Mr. Khalil Azad said, "Ms. Mo'tamed, do you want to work with a teacher who could answer all of your questions?" As if I was waiting for this, I responded, "Yes, why not?" He said, "There is someone called Sha'ban Ali Afifeh. He can answer anything you ask. Only that…" I asked, "Only what?" I was still in the dark. He said, "Mr. Afifeh intends to get married, and we have introduced you. He is going to propose to you." I hung my head down in embarrassment and was stunned. I grabbed my things hastily and headed back home.

I never thought about marriage, so I didn't take this proposal seriously. I talked with no one about it at home, neither my sister nor my parents. Before long, Farahnaz contacted me on the house phone. She said, "Don't do that. He is a very good guy. He is a longtime friend of my husband. We often visit each other. We know him well. He is a combatant, too. You said you liked combatants, right?" When she said 'combatant' I shuddered and knew I had to think twice. I called to mind the days at the Basij base when we were collecting donations and washing the clothes of the combatants on the frontline. I was always envious of them. I washed and ironed their bloodied clothes with love. I crocheted them shawls and hats. I packed dried figs for the combatants. I envied the fact that I wasn't a boy and could not go to the frontline. Farahnaz changed my mind with just this one word: combatant.

When I was alone with my mother, I told her everything. She informed *Aghajaan*. *Aghajaan* felt uncomfortable when he found out who my suitor was. "Don't ever mention it. We are very different. We don't even share kindred blood and are far away culturally," he said.

I never had the courage to talk to *Aghajaan* directly. I said to my mother, "Mom, you are offending God. Ali is a man of prayers and ethics. This should be enough for you." Seeing my insistence and conflict between *Aghajaan* and myself, my mother called my cousin, Gholam Hussein Eslampanah. He was busy gathering public donations for the frontline. He was a benevolent, warm-hearted person. He said, "I know him. He is a very good guy. I haven't seen him making a single mistake." He then paid us a visit and told *Aghajaan* about Ali's goodness and virtues. Hearing my cousin's words, *Aghajaan* went out to inquire about Ali further in the neighborhood, Masjid, IRGC base, and from everyone he knew.

Everyone said he was a nice guy and there was nothing wrong with him. He said to my mother, "The more I asked, the more people told me about his goodness. No one has ever dispraised him." Despite these acknowledgments, he still opposed our marriage because living with a combatant was hard, and he may be captured, become disabled, or martyred. Also, I was a sensitive girl and all of these factors could impact me severely. In the meantime, it was very important for *Aghajaan* that his son-in-law was to his liking, and Ali and his family were not his preference for me at all. "Our families are not made for each other," he said. When I found out that my insistence was not working, I resorted to my old tactic and started to abstain from eating again. When I was alone, I asked God to soften *Aghajaan*'s heart and make him change his mind. When we went to the mosque in the evenings, I only prayed to God to make *Aghajaan* change his mind regarding the proposal.

> *In the darkness of the night, she went by the howz and performed ablution. She spread her prayer rug and began saying her prayers. She was so keyed up inside. Her stomach was in knots. Only prayers and devotion could calm her down. She constantly read the Quran and recited dhikr.[24] She prayed to God under her breath, with her eyes full of tears. She wanted a man from God whom she had never seen. Her only reason for her tendency toward this marriage was that he was a combatant. The fact that he had sacrificed himself to go to the frontline had literally fascinated her. She prayed so much that*

---

24. *Talqin* consists of *dhikrs* or reminders about Islamic beliefs (monotheism, prophethood, resurrection, *imamate*, etc.), which is recited over a dead body before its burial in a particular manner. It is recommended to recite *talqin* for the dead.

she eventually calmed down. Her tears slid over her chador. She stood up for prayers.

All my days were full of solicitation, begging, insistence, and crying. Then suddenly, like a gift from God, *Aghajaan* consented and allowed them to come for the proposal ceremony. Maybe God was compassionate with me and sent some mediators to *Aghajaan* in order to convince him. Firstly, it was decided that Ali and I would meet and talk to each other.

Alone, she was sitting in the class, drawing her chador over her face and gazing at her book. She was restless and could hear her heart beating. At the time, Mr. Khalil Azad and Ali came in. She stood up and greeted them faintly. Mr. Khalil Azad left the room. She was alone with Ali. She couldn't start the conversation. Keeping her head down, she still hadn't seen Ali but was stunned by his words. Ali was talking about Hadiths (religious sayings and words of Prophet Muhammad (s) and Imams (a) and traditions). In her heart, Tooba was talking to God. She said, "O God, I wish we marry if you deem it fit." When her communication with God came to an

end, her heart trembled. She was ill at ease. She listened to Ali's voice, "I like my wife to wear hijab.[25] I have chosen you mainly because of your manner of clothing. I came to your Arabic class several times and followed you in the alley with my motorcycle. Your hijab and serenity attracted my attention. That's why I insisted so much. Don't I look familiar to you? Haven't you seen me riding a motorcycle?" She looked up and then down again. She was shy and couldn't even tell him that she hadn't seen him before. Seeing her silence, Ali smiled.

We talked a lot. "I had no intention to marry. I am a combatant. But my family insists on it, and more importantly, it is Prophet Muhammad's (s) tradition," Ali said. "I go to the frontline. I may be captured, disabled, or even martyred. Could you endure this?" he continued. I had butterflies

---

25. The term *hijab* is mainly used to refer to a religious covering in the presence of *non-mahram* men. To maintain *hijab*, women must cover their body and adornments from *non-mahram* men. Of course, they do not need to cover their hands up to the wrist and their faces.

in my stomach. My voice was trembling. But I firmly tried to say, "Yes."

Ali's words were being repeated in my head. Since that day, I became even more inclined towards this marriage. Hearing his voice, I had fallen more in love with him. I can't bring to mind what he had been wearing. I took a glance, maybe one second, maximum. Even so, I was happy that I insisted so much and managed to convince *Aghajaan*. I wished the clock ticked quicker. I was still worried about *Aghajaan*'s final say.

Ali had three sisters and three brothers. He was the first boy and the third child. His sisters had married, but his brothers had not. The youngest child was studying in secondary school. The brothers were one or two years apart from each other. His mother was a housewife, and his father was a shopkeeper—he owned a grocery store.

Ali came to our home along with his mother and two sisters, so that they could also see me. We talked again. There was no trembling either in my heart or my voice this time. I wasn't in a state of agitation anymore. I was relaxed and could speak easily.

We talked about ourselves and asked questions. I said, "Actually, my family set a very high amount of *mahr*,[26] say five hundred gold coins. In case they say anything about the *mahr*, you should not be concerned. If you go along with it, I will annul it after the wedding." Ali lowered his head and said, "Okay."

We had been sitting around the room: *Aghajaan*, my mother, Ali, his parents and sisters, their son-in-law, and Mr. Khalil Azad. As soon as they were going to bring up the *mahr*, *Aghajaan* said strictly, "Five-hundred coins." It shocked everyone. Their son-in-law was about to say something, but Ali said, "*Haj Agha*, I agree." Everyone turned toward Ali to look at him. I was anxious. I was afraid Ali's family would disagree. "*Haj Agha*, I want to marry your daughter and accept the *mahr* you just set," Ali reaffirmed. Hearing his words, I calmed down, and our secret about the *mahr* remained there up to the point where I annulled it. He never told his family what the story was. Ali's announcement about the *mahr* astonished everyone. When the discussions and glances finally faded, they talked about the date of

---

26. *Mahr* is the money paid or owed by the groom to the bride at the time of marriage.

the engagement ceremony. We chose Imam Reza's (a) birthday as its date.

The next day, Ali's sister, Zaman *Khanum*,[27] called. Zaman *Khanum* took permission from *Aghajaan* to go to Shiraz for shopping. Around the time when Ali came to propose to me, we had also gone to a proposal ceremony for Hamid. Their engagement ceremony was also on the same date as ours. We went to Shiraz together: Ali and I, Zaman *Khanum*, Hamid, and his wife. We took bus tickets and set off. When we arrived in Shiraz, we went to a motel. We booked a room for the women and another one for the men. We even ate lunch and dinner separately. After resting for a while, we went to the bazaar. Throughout the time we were together, I kept my head down. I wanted to take a look at him, but I was too shy. I never looked up in the street. This was a habit from my childhood. Once, he came to me and said, "Why do you look down so much?! You are troubling yourself." Later on, he told me, "Keep your head high, but keep your eyes to yourself. That's important."

---

27. *Khanum* (lady) is an honorific way in which Iranian men often address their wives. This is sometimes used to address women in general, as well.

That day, in any of the stores we went to, I rejected anything they were going to buy. "I have something like that; I don't need it," I said. At last, his sister felt offended due to my hesitation to shop. She said bitterly, "If you don't want to buy anything, why did we travel such a long way?" I can clearly remember that she opened her floral purse and said, "Look, we have brought along this money to buy things for you. We won't return home until we have spent it all." She had plenty of cash in her purse.

I said, "Actually, it's wartime now, and in such situations, I don't like to …". She interrupted me and said, "You are becoming a bride, you have to buy things." Long story short, I bought a wedding ring. Ali also bought an agate ring. And for everything else, I did what I had to. I couldn't find it in my heart to buy anything. My sister-in-law bought me whatever my brother's wife was buying without even asking: a bangle, a necklace, a wristwatch, a bracelet, a set of clothes, a *chador*, and a pair of shoes. We went into a wedding gown shop. "I don't want you to rent your bridal dress. I would like to buy it for you," he said. I was reticent, but I was very excited inside. We bought some white silk fabric with embossed flowers, as well as a veil and bridal crown. We got the gown sewn by the tailor. Prior to our wedding, I gave it to two other brides to wear for their own wedding ceremonies. I informed Ali that I was doing so. "I have bought it for you, if you want to, do as you wish," he said.

We returned to the motel after shopping and stayed in Shiraz for about a week. Ali was burning the midnight oil. He was studying for *konkur* (the university entrance exam).

In terms of financial status, Ali was at an average level. However, when it came to me, he went out of his way. I was raised in a financially sound family. We were never short of anything. Despite that, I was not a materialistic person and never wanted anything from Ali. He always said to his friends, "I wish she would once ask me to buy her something."

> *They were sitting shoulder to shoulder. Others were rubbing sugar cones together above their heads.[28] Tooba was holding the Quran in her*

---

28. Rubbing suger canes over the bride and groom is an Iranian wedding custom, as an emblem of conferring sweetness to their lives.

hands and was lip-reading Surah Maryam.²⁹ The Alim (religious notary) was also reading the verse to sanctify their wedding. She said, "Yes" on the third repetition, just like most other brides.³⁰ At that moment, she prayed for everyone to have prosperity in life. Others were blissed out, clapping and throwing out noghl,³¹ lollies, and sugars. Tooba closed the Quran and held it against her forehead. She closed her eyes and wished that God would give her patience. She was anxious inside, but relied on God and kissed the Quran.

On August 28, 1984, Mr. Ayatollahi, Lar's³² Imam Jom'a,³³ solemnized our

---

29. The 19th chapter of the Holy Quran.

30. It is traditional that during wedding ceremonies, the bride consents to the marriage on the third call by the notary.

31. *Noql* is a small confectionary produced in various sizes and flavors. In Iran, *noql* is a symbol of happiness. There is an old tradition of throwing *noqls* on the bride and groom in weddings.

32. Lar is an ancient city in southern Iran. It is located 330 kilometers in southeastern Shiraz.

33. *Imam Jum'a* or Imam of Friday Prayer, is a person who leads the Friday prayers. He is appointed by the religious ruler.

marriage in the marriage registry bureau. Then, we returned home. We had arranged a very modest wedding table-spread. Bread and honey are all I remember of it. That night, we put on our wedding rings and ate honey. At the end of the ceremony, all of the relatives went home, even the groom. My aunt said, "The groom should have stayed; at least he should have spoken to the bride for a few minutes!" But I didn't mind. I went into the room, laid out my prayer rug, and read the rest of *Surah Maryam*.

In the morning, I woke up to the sound of *Aghajaan* praying. I performed ablution (*wudhu*) and started to recite my prayers. *Aghajaan* had a bad accident when I was a child. I couldn't recall anything about it. My mother, however, said that there was almost no hope he would survive at all. But it was Allah's will for *Aghajaan* to have a longer life. After that accident, my mother always performed two-*raka'ah*[34] prayers for *Aghajaan* to remain in the best of health, and so did I, when I grew up. But, in addition to *Aghajaan*'s health, I recited two-*raka'ah*

---

34. *Rak'ah* is a unit of the prayer, which includes standing (*qiyām*), *rukū'*, and two prostrations (*sajdah*).

prayers for the health of my husband, too. I prayed for him to be under the protection of Almighty God wherever he was.

From that day on, every time someone knocked on our door, I thought it might be Ali. But it was not. They had no telephone at home. His sisters had telephones in their homes, but they had been married and lived away from their family. I was completely out of touch with him on the first and second day. I was missing him immensely and the images of our wedding day kept running through my mind. On the third day, when *Aghajaan* came home for lunch, Ali also came along with him. He was too shy to come alone. He went to *Aghajaan*'s shop, and *Aghajaan* had invited him for lunch. In our engagement period, he rarely came to our home to visit alone. Most of the time, he went to *Aghajaan*'s shop and came home with him. When I saw Ali, I went to put on my black-colored *chador* and came to sit by him.

When I went out to perform ablution at prayer time, I picked up a damask rose from the garden and put it in his pocket. I tried to give him a flower whenever he came to our home. Ali also kept the flower in his pocket when he stood to say his prayers.

I laid out his prayer rug myself, the first time he said his prayers in our home. I told him, "When we are together, I would like to lay out your prayer rug myself, my dear." After we were married whenever we were together alone, I called him 'my dear.' After lunch, he asked for a toothpick. He had a gap between his teeth. The food got lodged in that gap whenever he ate something and it bothered him. I fetched him the toothpick. From that day on, I always remembered to put a few toothpicks inside his pocket before eating. "How don't you lose sight of that?!" he always asked. "When you are in love, you will remember everything," I replied.

We had lunch and went into the yard. He stood beside me as I was washing the dishes. I never let him wash the dishes. "Doing it alone will take longer; this way, we can talk more," I said. Then, I brought out my Arabic book and asked all of my questions, one by one. Ali answered all my questions. I was so bright-eyed and bushy-tailed. A few days later, I was invited for lunch by my mother-in-law. Ali came in a Toyota to collect me. He drove very smoothly when we were together. However, according to his friends, when he was in the frontlines or with them, he would step on the gas so hard that they constantly hit their heads against the car's roof. But he was always cautious behind the wheel when he was with me. Sometimes, I looked at him for so long that he smiled and said, "Look ahead!"

Ali and his family lived in the old Lar, in a small, and austere home. Overall, there was a kitchen and a room, maybe a total of thirty square meters. They had no bathroom and went to the public bath. In their small yard, there were a few chickens, roosters, and a goat. Whenever I went to their home, his mother milked the goat for us to drink.

Two weeks after our wedding, one of Ali's relatives held a wedding party. Ali came by, and we went there. When the party was over, we got in the car, so he could take me home. He was about to say something, but he was in a quandary. Finally, he poured his heart out. Over these two weeks, I wore the *chador* and brought my books whenever Ali came around. "Tooba, you are my wife. Why do you wear your *chador* in front of me?" he questioned. He kept on talking about it for quite a while, and I only listened. When he was finished, I turned toward him and said, "You are very rude!" He said nothing. He only smiled. Neither of us talked anymore on the way. Ali took me to the desert. We both got out of the car. He pointed at the mountains and said, "We get trained here." It was interesting for me. I was pretty fond of hearing these stories.

The next time he came round, I did not wear the chador. He looked at me and smiled. I didn't bring my books either. We talked about our married life. He mostly came to give me a ride in the afternoons. If we were five minutes late, my mother and *Aghajaan* became worried and waited by the front door. One day, when I was at their home, Ali said, "Let's go take a look at our house, which is under construction." So, I got back home about ten minutes late. My mother had come down to the end of the alley. *Aghajaan* was also at the front door. When we arrived, they told Ali, "You said you were going to get back at such and such time. You are ten minutes late. That worried us." Ali apologized, "Sorry, it won't happen again," he said. My mother and *Aghajaan* loved Ali. Despite the fact that *Aghajaan* was a staunch opponent of our marriage, he now took a liking to Ali so much that you couldn't believe he had ever opposed him. Apart from my family, Ali was in the heart of my relatives and was talked about trendily. They used to invite us to their houses a lot. Ali was invited twice to the supplication of *Kumayl*[35] ceremony at my aunt's and her son's houses. He read over the supplication and eulogized at the ceremony. He had a tuneful voice. Sometimes, we went to the martyr's cemetery for the supplication of *Nodbeh*[36] on Fridays. It was very soothing, and I felt amazing.

Ali would sometimes travel to Bandar Abbas[37] to bring fish back to Lar for sale. He loaded the fish into the back of the Toyota pickup truck and covered them with crushed ice to prevent their spoilage. At night, he went to the mosque. At the Basij base, he trained the boys from the neighbourhood and sent them to the frontline.

I was talking to him over the phone once and noticed how happy he was. I inquired

---

35. The supplication of *Kumayl* is a mystical supplication, which Imam ʿAli (a) taught Kumayl b. Ziyad, a close companion of his. It is commonly recited by Shias, particularly on Thursday nights.
36. The *Nodbeh* Supplication is a prayer whereby one cries out for the occultation of Imam al-Mahdi (a). Shias often recite this supplication in Friday mornings.
37. Bandar Abbas is a port city in southern Iran, where the biggest container port of Iran is located.

about it, "I passed the university entrance exam, Tooba!" he replied. I got excited. He had been accepted at Tabriz University in Agricultural Engineering. But my happiness was only short-lived. When I hung up the phone, I realized that he would go to Tabriz, and I had to stay alone. It depressed me.

The autumn started as he left for Tabriz. Before leaving, he came to visit us at home for farewells. My mother put some packs of pistachio and sunflower seeds in his suitcase. I passed the Quran over his head; he kissed it. I also spilled water on the ground behind his back.[38] After saying goodbye, I closed the door and broke down in tears. Before long, I missed him. I behaved like a crazy person. Everyone could understand how much I loved him. At nights, I cried up to the point that I fell asleep. My pillow was always wet from my tears—both during the engagement period when I lived with my parents, as well as after the wedding when I was in his mother's house.

He called once or twice a week. When my endurance ran out, I called his sister and

---

38. Spilling water behind the traveler is an ancient Iranian tradition. It was carried out as an expression of hope for his or her safe return.

asked her about Ali. She always said, "He is alright, don't worry." Ali returned to Lar the following January. He said he had taken six different vehicles to arrive in Lar. "Tabriz is very cold. The cold air cracks the skin," he said. During the few days he stayed in Lar, he was either in the Basij base or IRGC base. He visited me only if he had time.

Chapter 3

A Difficult Promise

Ali's departure left me with nothing but gloom again. His phone calls were my only delight. One day, he called and said he was going to go to the frontline. "I have promised not to argue with you about it. So, go. I wish you Godspeed." I said. We could barely talk to each other over the phone whenever he went to the frontline, even less than when he was at the university. We only greeted each other. He always said, "It's a long line here. Others are also waiting to call. It's better we keep our conversation short."

Days were passing one by one. Spring was on its way again; spring of 1985. It was the first Nowruz since Ali had set foot into my life and had become the man of my dreams. Spring had arrived; Ali didn't though. It was operation time, and he had to stay at the frontline. I was on edge. I read the Quran constantly to calm myself. At the moment of the turn of the year, Hamid and his wife, as well as my sister and her husband and children, gathered at our home. Once I caught a glimpse of my brother with his wife, my mind wandered back to that day in Shiraz when we were together. I became so gloomy. I thought to myself, "Why shouldn't Ali be with me right now?" I couldn't stand it. I grabbed my clothes to take a shower.

> *She turned on the faucet and sat in the corner of the bath. She put her hand on her heart, and tears filled her eyes. In the sound of water, her sobs drowned. She was heavy-hearted. It was Eid, and her man was not by her side. She was suffering from loneliness. She yearned for Ali to come back soon, and she could pour her heart out to him. She was crying profusely. When she stopped crying, she splashed water onto her face.*

I wore my *chador* and went to visit my mother-in-law. I wished them a happy New Year and went back home. During the first week of the Eid holidays, we had guests every single day. My aunts, relatives, friends, and neighbors would pay a visit. As usual, when the Eid visiting ceremonies ended, we made our way to the desert. I was depressed and didn't spend time with anyone. I was desperately feeling in need of Ali. I had leaned against a boulder and lowered my head, minding my own business. Meanwhile, Ziba came, holding a camera and said, "Tooba, keep your head up; I'm going to take a photo of you." I didn't move. She took a sad, broken-hearted photo of me and went away. I still have that photo. After returning to Lar, they informed us that Ali had been injured and admitted to the Mustafa Khomeini Hospital in Isfahan. Worriedly, I called the hospital. "Tooba, I'm OK, don't worry," he said. That was a relief when I found out he was fine. From that day on, I kept calling the hospital in the morning, noon, and evening to talk to Ali.

Two weeks passed by. One day, Mrs. Alavi, my school principal, dropped by. She asked about Ali. "He's been injured and hospitalized," I said. "Do you know which part of his body has been injured?" she asked. "His hand," I replied. "What if his hand becomes infected and has to be cut off?" she said. "Hazrat Abu al-Fazl[39] (a) also had his hand lost in the battle. I have promised Ali to stay by his side every second of my life, even if he gets captured or hurt," I answered. Later on, Mrs. Alavi said that her brother had seen Ali in the hospital and found out about his hand. Her brother had asked her to tell me about it somehow and put a spin on it. Mrs. Alavi did what her brother had asked, but I didn't get the message.

During those days, I regularly visited my mother-in-law. Sometimes, she invited me for dinner. That night, their house was quiet, like always. They were aware of what had happened but tried to act normally. They didn't want me to find out anything. When we had dinner, I took all the dishes to the kitchen. I took my wedding ring out and set it aside. Since I didn't want it to become dirty, I always took it off when doing chores. After doing the dishes, I went back home. Upon arriving home, I came to know that I had misplaced my ring in their house. My

---

39. 'Abbas (647-680), known as Abu al-Fazl and Qamar Bani Hashim, was the son of Imam 'Ali (a) and Umm al-Baneen. He was the commander and flag-bearer of Imam al-Husayn's army in the Event of Karbala.

mother said, "I'll go fetch it tomorrow." She went in the morning and brought it back. When she returned, she began speaking strangely, just like Mrs. Alavi. I thought to myself, "First Mrs. Alavi and now mom; clearly, they must be hiding something from me!" My mother constantly told me about Hazrat Abu al-Fazl (a). I was quite sure that something must have happened to Ali's hand. I was in a sweat. I felt like yelling out, "I am Ali's wife; when all of you know it, why shouldn't I know? Why would he keep it from me?" He hadn't told me any lies, though. He had just kept the truth hidden. I always thought Ali was true to me. I never imagined he would hide anything from me. I was in a huff, heartbroken. I picked up the phone and called the hospital. When I heard Ali's voice, I poured out all of my heart in one sentence, "I have heard you've injured your hand." I blurted out. "So?" he said. "Shouldn't I have found out earlier? Why didn't you tell me during the last two weeks?" I questioned. "I'm really proud of you for having lost your hand at the frontline, my dear," I continued. Hearing this, he erupted in laughter and said, "I have lost my hand, and you're proud of it?!" I said, "Well, I am your wife! I've been granted the gift of living with a disabled veteran.

I want to come to Isfahan." He asked me not to do so. I insisted. Ali said, "My dear, it will not be ideal for you to visit me here." I was not convinced. I asked my mother and *Aghajaan* to allow me to travel to Isfahan to see Ali. "He told you not to go there. Why do you insist so much on going?" they said. I decided to ask Ziba to call Ali and tell him that Tooba was on her way to Isfahan. I intended to go if he did not object. I sat beside my sister. I stuck my ear to the phone in her hand. Ali showed no anger when Ziba told him I was to visit with Hamid. He seemed glad to hear it. When she almost hung up the phone, I jumped into the air and said "Hooray!" so loudly that everyone stared at me. I ran to put on my clothes. Among the members of Ali's family, Ezzat's husband also came with me. Haj Abbas, my brother, and I set off together.

It took us about seventeen to eighteen hours to reach Isfahan from Lar. We took a bus to Shiraz and then a taxi to Isfahan from there. We arrived at 2 or 3 p.m. I did not even care about the beauties of Isfahan. I was only looking around to find the hospital. It was Friday,[40] and we were free to make a visit at any time.

---

40. Friday is the official weekend according to the Iranian calendar.

Holding the vase in her hand, she climbed the stairs two at a time. She had come a long way, counting every second to see Ali. Every time Ali used to come to see her, this time, it was her turn. She was looking around to find his room, and she finally did. "Is Ali really in this room?" She held the vase tight. Puffing and panting, she went through. On the doorstep, she turned her eyes to look inside the room. Her eyes were glued to Ali's. She was in a complete daze. How frail he had become! Skin-and-bones! Pale as a ghost. The hair on his head was all shaved off. She could not believe it. Was he her Ali?! Her hands started to shake. She squeezed her chador in her hand. Then, she swallowed the lump in her throat, raised a smile, stepped in, and stood by Ali's bed. Greeted him and put the vase on the bedside table. Then, she pushed aside the blanket and bent to kiss the stump of his amputated hand. She got a fix on the stitches on Ali's throat and kissed them, too. "I have to kiss your scars one by one," she said. A teardrop fell on the ground from the corner of her eye. She smiled. Ali smiled too. They had desperately missed each other. What a hard time they had. How

little their chance was to see each other. Both of them were longing for nothing more than just to sit and hold a gaze at one another!

There were two very sick, injured veterans in the room. One of them was in an awful condition. His skin was scaling in large flakes. Another one had been shell-shocked and poisoned with chemicals. He was constantly yelling and roaring. He was also bare-skinned and was covered only by a sheet. He yelled at the top of his voice, "Commander! Where are you? They are ready to attack! When will the ammo arrive?" He was suffering tremendously and was martyred a few days later. Ali had one of his hands cut off, and they had pulled out shell fragments from his body. Ali was in a better condition than the other two.

I was there with him for only thirty-three hours. I stayed even longer than I was supposed to. They were constantly bringing-over the war-injured patients. The hospital was overcrowded. They were continuously announcing that the patients' companions should leave. Whenever the doctors came, I hid in the room next door. Also, sometimes I hid under the bed. I enjoyed being alongside Ali despite all these difficulties. I was eager to help him as much as I could, during these moments of togetherness. I fed him, assisted him in performing ablution, and arranged his prayer mat.

Hamid and Haj Abbas came at night. They were so tired that they soon dozed off. Hamid fell asleep sitting on the seat and leaning his head on the bed. Haj Abbas also spread a sheet on the floor and slept on it. We felt like talking to each other. But we did not want to bother anyone with our whispers. "Let's go into the yard," Ali said. I picked up his serum, and we went out silently. In the yard, we walked together a little bit. There were tall trees in the middle of the yard and rows of seats on both sides. The breeze blew on our faces as we walked. We were enjoying ourselves. We sat on one of the seats. From that night forward, I called him 'Abu al-Fazl'.[41]

"Abu al-Fazl! Not even all the people on earth can separate us." I said, fixing my eyes on him. "One of my friends burnt his face a little in an operation. His fianceé, who was his

---

41. In the history of Karbala, Hazrat Abu al-Fadl lost his hands, and from that moment on, veterans, in particular those whose hands are injured in war, are given the honorofic name 'Abu al-Fadl'.

cousin, said that she did not want to be with him anymore and they should get divorced. I was scared I might have lost you, Tooba! When I regained consciousness and found that I had lost my hand, I never said, 'Oh! My hand!' I said, 'Oh, Tooba!'" he told me.

"Why did these thoughts cross your mind? Hadn't we talked before our marriage regarding this? Don't you remember I said I would be patient even if you became disabled, caught, or martyred?" I asked.

"I know, but I was still worried despite all that," he said.

That night at the hospital was the first time we were speaking warmly from the heart. Alongside all of the things we talked about, I never mentioned I was upset over his dishonesty and secrecy. Later in Lar, I had a conversation with him about it, heart-to-heart.

Ali was a man-of-all-work at the frontline, from the battalion's deputy commander to the ambulance driver. He did everything that should have been done. On the day of the accident, he had been taking a few injured veterans to the rear when their ambulance was hit by a rocket. When they were taking him to the hospital, his hand had been connected to his body only by skin. I always thought it was God's blessing. If that skin had been cut off, they would have removed the skin from his leg to graft it to his hand.

Neither my mom nor *Aghajaan* wanted me to get a divorce. All of my family loved Ali. We were all proud that he was with us and joyful that we had him. During the seventeen or eighteen days that Ali was in the hospital, many tried to separate us. They called or came to our house. They would say, "Are you really going to live with someone who has lost his hand!? Do you know how difficult that is? Do you know what that means?" It was heartbreaking to hear those words. I wanted to shout at them and tell them that Ali had lost his hand so that we could live in comfort. I was always tongue-tied but once, when one of the relatives said, "You were ill-omened. Ali has been going to the frontline for years; why hadn't he been injured so far?" I could no longer tolerate it and said, "God intended to divide his rewards in two; one half for him and one half for his wife so that he doesn't get all the rewards for himself!" They literally could not understand me. They could not comprehend what I meant. On the very first day, when Ali talked about becoming disabled or martyred, I found out he would not stay with me. But I wanted to live alongside him, even for a short time.

Reproaches and rumors were circulating; I didn't care, though. I was just counting the seconds to see Ali back in Lar. Two operations were performed on his hand in the hospital. Finally, he came back with the same vase I had given him. I found that my love for him increased as I saw the vase in his hand. He had brought the vase to Lar with his only hand. *Aghajaan* had bought a sheep to sacrifice for him.[42] We held a party at my mother-in-law's house. They bought the rice and desserts, and we brought the sheep and chicken. That night, I stayed with him. When everyone went to sleep, Ali said, "Put your head on my residual limb. I want you to really feel that my arm is gone." I was against it. He insisted, and I finally agreed.

She was in turmoil. She had a deep-rooted feeling of aversion toward it, but Ali had insisted upon it. Slowly, she bent her head and placed it on his shoulder. She

---

42. The costum of sacrificing sheep at the return of someone after a long time being on a trip is to welcome a person back in their home usually after a long journey (like Hajj) or event.

felt a tight sensation in her throat when she sensed the bandage wrapped around his arm. The reproaches and dressing-downs were haunting her like a trauma as she dug into it. "You were ill-omened; he has lost his hand; how are you going to live with him?" She burst into tears all of a sudden. Ali heard her crying. He knew how mournful she was. Tooba had never revealed her feelings, but he had read her through her eyes.

I stayed with Ali's family for a couple of days. The doctor had prescribed oiling and massaging under his armpit several times to avoid the growth of soft-tissue deficits. So, I regularly did that for him. I laid out his prayer rug and helped him with his clothes. I buttoned up his shirt for him, even before he became disabled. I had learned it from my mother; she always sprayed perfumes on *Aghajaan*'s coats, dressed him, and combed his hair. She would also always polish and shine his shoes. Before his injury, he never prevented me from doing that. He only thanked me for it. But now, he insisted, "I want to do it myself." I smiled and kept on doing it. He threw me a side-glance and said, "Please don't do it, my dear. If I don't get used to this state, I cannot do it in the university or at the frontline." Sometimes, he smiled and tapped on my hand gently, saying, "Please stop it." On the third day at their home, *Aghajaan* came by to take me home. After that day, he never let me stay at their home again. "Go see your fiancé for a few hours and come back," he said. I went, visited Ali, and came back. I loved to be with Ali, but *Aghajaan* would not allow it.

The days flew by, and the month of Ramadan arrived. I climbed up our palm tree to pick dates off the stalks for Ali. He ate those dates for *iftar*. "I have picked them with my own hands!" I said. I never let him see how I climbed the palm tree, it would embarrass me. My mother, sisters, and I went to the mosque during the *Qadr* nights.[43] I always prayed that these difficult days of separation would soon be over. God brought our separation to an end soon and provided

---

43. *Laylat al-Qadr* is otherwise known as the Night of Power and is considered to be the Islamic calendar's holiest eve. During this night, Angel Jibril revealed the Holy Qur'an's first verses to Prophet Muhammad. This is a night of great commemoration and devotion to Allah (swt) and placed higher than that of one thousand months.

another pathway for us. On the *Eid al-Fitr*[44] of the same year, we went to their home to pay a visit. Ali was hinting that I should stay with him that night. I was also making faces to explain that *Aghajaan* would not let me stay and that it was not my fault. On our way back, we also visited relatives and friends and finally went to the martyrs' cemetery. He called me on the phone in the afternoon, "You let me down since you did not stay. I have talked to my family. I have decided to hold a wedding ceremony for you." I got happy and told my mother. She also informed *Aghajaan*. "We have no problem with that. Let them do what they should for the wedding ceremony," *Aghajaan* said. My dowry was ready. *Aghajaan* and my mother constantly went to the bazaar, purchased things, and stored them in the cellar; a refrigerator, gas stove, vacuum cleaner, etc. I was never a person that needed to have so many things. However, *Aghajaan* went out of his way for me. Everything was ready, and we only awaited the house maintenance activities to be complete. In the meantime, we didn't linger over that. We pushed on so

---

44. The *Eid* which marks the end of the month of Ramadan.

much that the tile work was finished the day after our wedding. Yard maintenance was also still up in the air.

A few days before the wedding, Ali brought his suit and asked me to shorten and fit his trouser legs. We decided that I would shorten and hem one leg and get him to sew the other one. He could do many of his daily chores, even though he only had one hand. He was wonderful. I put the leg of his trousers on my knees and started to make delicate zigzag stitches. I thought to myself, "I have to do it so beautifully that Ali appreciates me and my skills, in a way that his mother and sisters also give me credit for it!" As it was finished, when I intended to take it high and make a show of it, I realized that I had sewn the edge of the trouser leg to my own trousers! Ali burst out laughing in such a way that I'll never forget it. We were both laughing loudly. We were so happy together that we could barely think of our hardships. "Tooba! I sewed it better than you, with only one hand!" he said.

Chapter 4

Hand in a Prosthetic Hand at Our Wedding

On the wedding night, Ali's sisters took me to the beauty salon. It was agreed that they would pick me up at eight o'clock. We were three brides there, and I was the first one to be attended to. It was *adhan*[45] time. "I'm going to recite my prayers," I said. "If so, you will become the second bride to receive makeup, so you will be ready later," the makeup artist said. "They are going to take us. So, what's the problem with doing it one hour later?" I replied. Since the appointment time was delayed, Ali's sisters couldn't collect me, and Hamid took on the role. It was not

---

45. *Adhan* is a call for Muslims, which informs them of the time of prayer.

customary for the groom to come and pick up the bride. When I got into the car, I held my head down because they were bringing the martyrs' bodies. I was embarrassed. On the other hand, I did not like to be pointed at and called a 'bride' by people. I had my *chador* on, but still, I didn't want anyone to see me. When we arrived home, Ali came by. In the city of Lar, when the groom comes in, the bride takes his hand. I reached out and took Ali's hand. My heart skipped a beat; Ali's hand was firm! I had put on my chador, and I could not see him well. I thought he would offer his right hand, but it was obviously his left one. I finally found out that he had a prosthetic hand. Everyone came over to congratulate us. Late at night, *Aghajaan* and my mother kissed us goodbye and held the Quran above our heads. Our house was about eighty square meters. Ali's father's shop was on our house's left side. We had set up an aluminum door in our yard, which was opened toward his shop so that he could come and go easily in case he needed to. We had an unfinished ten-square-meter earthy yard. The yard led to the kitchen. The bath was also inside the kitchen. Before the entrance of the room, there was a door with a staircase behind it. The stairs led to the roof. We had some closets on some corners of our L-shaped room and had installed curtains on the other side to separate it into two rooms, so that I could go about easily when we had male guests.

Half-asleep, I drew the curtain to go to the kitchen the morning after our wedding. I suddenly came across something very frightening. I screamed and put my hand on my heart. Ali woke up from my scream and said, "What happened?!" agitatedly. I pointed at his prosthetic hand lying on the floor in the middle of the room. "I saw your prosthetic hand and got scared. I thought it was a real one," I faltered. "I'm sorry, I shouldn't have left it there," he apologized, upsettedly. I put the kettle on. Whenever Ali and I were alone, we never drank tea. Instead, we drank boiling water. The story of breaking off from tea had to do with me. I was a high school student, and I had a test. I was studying the books so hard when suddenly I spilled the hot teacup on my hand. I, therefore, burnt my hand so badly that I decided to put drinking tea aside for good. During our engagement period, finding out that I didn't drink tea anymore, Ali said, "When my wife does not drink tea, why should I? I won't drink either." He only sipped tea at the parties as a sign of respect to others. When the water boiled, I prepared breakfast, and we ate it together. When I finished the dishes, I put my wedding dress on again, and we took some photos with my mother-in-law and sisters-in-law.

On the first day of marriage, *Aghajaan* sacrificed a sheep. He marinated the pieces of meat with yogurt and onion and brought them over for us. It's a type of kebab specific to our city called *Kenjeh*. We made that kebab hoping that the relatives on both sides would become more intimate and closer. Ali and I ate from one kebab skewer, and the rest were distributed among his relatives.

A few days later, Ali began repairing the yard. He hired a bricklayer and also assisted him in the job. They paved the yard and carved scenery of nature on the wall. Recovering from the fatigue of the construction activity, one day, he bought *Kalle-Pache*[46] and came home around sundown. We cleaned and washed it together. We poured the *Kalle-Pache* into a pot and deep-cooked it overnight. When

---

46. *Kalle-Pache* is a traditional dish made with sheep's head and limbs. This is a popular high-calorie food in Iran, which is often served for breakfast.

I woke up to say my morning prayers, the smell of *Kalle-Pache* had pervaded the entire house. The sun had yet to rise. I took half of the *Kalle-Pache* to my mother-in-law's house. "I couldn't find it in my heart to eat it without you," I told her. That was the most delicious one I have eaten in my whole life.

We decided to invite our families over to our home. I was a good cook. When I was single, my sisters and I took turns cooking, washing dishes, crushing sugar cubes, and so on. Therefore, I was skilled in housework. We had invited lots of guests, but it was not difficult for me at all. I cleaned the chickens and soaked the rice. When furnishing our home with my dowry, the large trays and pots were placed in the storeroom above the bathroom. We did not have a ladder. "What should we do, Ali?" I asked. He looked at me and pointed at his shoulders. "Get on my shoulders and bring the pots down," he said. He bent down. I climbed up his shoulders to reach up for the pots. I was laughing, and so was he. I brought the pots down. He was my ladder whenever the need arose. When the curtain was ready to be installed, I went up on his shoulders again. That day, my mother-in-law and sisters-in-law came by to give me a hand. We prepared food, and our families gathered around. That night, the party was fun, and we had a good night, as I had hoped. We held parties and had recreational activities outdoors, too. Mostly, we went to the desert at the weekends. My family used to hang out a lot. We would go on outings for any reason. Sometimes, we prepared lunch at home and took it with us. But other times, when we decided to go out all at once, we cooked the meal down at our campsite. We didn't care whether it was hot or cold; we did our thing. We grabbed our necessities and went for the picnic. One of these camping days was bitterly cold. I shivered every now and then. Ali knew I was cold, even without me saying anything. He took off his overcoat and draped it over my shoulders.

We went to the house of Mr. Molaei, Ali's friend, most nights, . After finishing my activities in the mosque and the Basij base, I stayed with Mr. Molaei's wife, Ali and Mr. Molaei went to work in the pastry shop. They had five or six children of all ages. Ali used to finish work and come pick me up late at night. Sometimes, it was eleven-thirty or twelve o'clock, and sometimes even one or two o'clock in the morning. We were only delighted by these parties and camping activities.

I loved the idea of going to Mashhad [47]with Ali, but it never happened. He was too busy to go on a trip. I was six when I first went to Mashhad. Our relatives had come to visit us at home; we were supposed to travel to Mashhad to visit Imam Reza's (a) shrine that night. We, the children, were playing with water in the yard. We were actively engaged in playing, but I suddenly realized that my sister Zhila was drowning in the water and had suffered from water aspiration. I called out to my mom worriedly. Zhila had fainted. All of us were crying. My mother went to call the workers in the street for help. They came over and helped us take Zhila to the hospital. We were so scared and panicked that all of us went barefoot. Although I was a kid, I called out to Imam Reza (a) for help several times. I had seen the grownups always seeking help from him. Zhila had finally recovered, and we went to Mashhad that very night. It was a good trip. We took a group photo. Now, the memories of those days were so alive in my mind that

---

47. Mashhad is a city in northeastern Iran, located in the center of Razavi Khorasan Province. The city is home to the mausoleum of Imam al-Ridha (a), the eighth Shiite Imam.

I was giving in to the temptation of paying a visit to Imam Reza's (a) shrine. My family had booked tickets to Mashhad. Ali insisted that I go with my family. "No! If we are to go, we're going together." I insisted. "I can't come. You know how busy I am," he said. "So, we'll go whenever you're not tied up," I said. However, the occasion never arose. I will remain forever pining about visiting Imam Reza (a) with Ali.

He was exhausted when he came home. But he tried to pretend otherwise. He smiled more. I understood him very well and tried to help him as much as possible at home. I peeled oranges and apples for him. I never gave him pomegranates with peels; I always deseeded them in a bowl. He was an appreciative person. He always tried to return the favor. Coming back from grocery shopping, he helped me with cutting and slicing meat and chicken. He was also assisting in washing and packaging them. If I happened to cut my finger, he brought out band-aids hastily, covered my wound, and did the rest of the chores. He would not let me do anything. "I'm okay," I reassured him. "No need, I'm doing it. It's almost done," he said. One day, when he was finished with the housework, he came and sat beside me. "Okay, now it's my turn to bring an unfinished business to a close. Let's go to the marriage registry bureau. I'm going to nullify the five hundred gold coins of my *mahr*. I will only keep five of them for the Five Holy Ones,"[48] I said.

The next morning we went to the marriage registry bureau. Mr. Sheikh al-Eslami was sitting behind the desk. When I told him the story, he asked me to take a seat. He called *Aghajaan*, but he assumed I didn't realize that. He told *Aghajaan* everything subtly. From his mannerism, I found out how furious *Aghajaan* had become. "Since she wants to do this without my permission, she is no longer my daughter!" *Aghajaan* had told him. I breathed a sigh of relief as I signed the marriage document. In the evening, I decided to go and visit *Aghajaan*. I was anxious. *Aghajaan* did not like it if

---

48. Prophet Muhammad (s), his daughter Lady Fatimah (a), his son-in-law Imam 'Ali (a), and his grandchildren Imam al-Hasan (a) and Imam al-Husayn (a) are known among the Shia as the Five Persons of the Clock (*Al-e 'Aba*) or *Ahl al-Kisa*.

anyone failed to heed his words, but I had to deliver my promise to Ali. Although he used to pretend he did not care, I had to stand by my word. *Aghajaan* was not home. I told my mother everything. She remained silent. Following that day, I felt afraid of confronting *Aghajaan* and tried to keep myself out of his sight. I missed him terribly. But his behavior kept me from facing up to him. I once saw him from a far distance in the street. I yearned for him immediately. "Agha!" I exclaimed spontaneously. He did not hear me. I was just watching him walk away. I do not know why I could not have my cake and eat it too.

Ali and I spent only one Ramadan together. It was extremely hot during those days. On the roof, he built a room out of clay and cement. I arranged the tablecloth for *iftar* and *suhoor* in that room. We had to climb lots of stairs to eat there, but Ali felt like having *iftar* and *suhoor* in the open, cool air, so I managed with the difficulties. I did not let him meddle with the preparation of *suhoor* or arranging the tablecloth. I did it all by myself and then woke him up. When it came to cleaning the dishes, I could not stop him. He would take the dishes down. It was so pleasant to eat by his side in that little room with that big, unglazed window. A cool breeze brushed our faces, alleviating the heat. One night, he came home about two or three hours after *Maghreb adhan*. I had not even eaten the food, and I was waiting for him. When he came and saw the uneaten food, he said, "Tooba, I went to pay my mom a visit after work. They stood firm that I had to eat my *iftar* there. I declined because I knew you would not eat anything alone." I smiled and said, "Would I ever break my fast without you?"

Ali was worried about my loneliness. He said, "You are alone at home, and I'm outdoors most of the time. It would be great if you further your education. This may lower my worries a bit." I had not obtained my diploma yet. After going to the seminary, returning to Lar, and failing to pass the final exams and the Arabic classes, I had totally given up on getting my diploma. He was now encouraging me to do it. He also tried to find out about it later. I preferred studying commerce at the university. However, in our city, they did not deliver commerce courses. Ali did not have time, so I went to Shiraz with my mother-in-law to track it in Shiraz's Education Bureau. The books had changed, and it was hard for me to go to Shiraz for classes. So I dropped the idea altogether. We came back home late at night. I was so tired that I went to bed and fell asleep as soon as my head touched the pillow. In the morning, I went into the kitchen and lost my head over the *halva*⁴⁹ Ali was cooking. He had stood there with a spatula in his hand. I was so thrilled that I bent down and kissed his hand. I expressed my deep love for him by praising him endlessly that day. He meant a lot to me. With his only hand, he mixed the flour for a long time to make *halva* for me. He knew how much I loved *halva*.

In September, universities opened again, and Ali should have left for Ardabil. He had taken leave the past semester due to his injury. And now, he made a transfer request to Ardabil. I grabbed my belongings and moved to my mother-in-law's house. We both had hard times. My tears dropped involuntarily every time I tried to eat. I wasn't used to fixing my plate before Ali's. I thought to myself, "Has he eaten anything

---

49. *Halva* is a well-known Iranian confectionary, made of wheat flour, oil, and sugar. Iranians often distribute this confectionary to their neighbors' homes or with the recitation of *al-Fateha* on the graves of their deceased ones.

yet? What did he eat?" Seeing my impatience and unrest, Ali's mother constantly said, "Don't do it to yourself; he'll be back soon." Ali's paternal grandmother lived with them. She was a very good woman, kind and sympathetic. She would sit beside me, caress me, and make me calm. She told me stories of her life and noted that the days of separation would come to an end soon. Ali would come back, and I would forget about all of those difficult times.

I had learned a lot in life; for example, I should stand by my husband in the worst of situations. This way, I would be a great comfort to him, and he would reciprocally be the same to me. I could not go to the frontline; he would say it was out of the question. But instead, I should have been able to go to Ardabil! When he returned home this time, I stood my ground to go with him to Ardabil. He said, "It's very cold there; you'll trouble yourself. It's a no-go." But I stood firm. "I don't care about the cold air! Being together is the only thing that matters. You are either at university or at the frontline; when can we be together then?" I said. I finally managed to persuade him to take me with him. I packed our clothes into the suitcase. I packaged everything that may have been needed, such as lentils, beans, peas, spices, and so on. We flew to Tehran, and from there, we took a bus to Ardabil. It was a twelve-hour journey. It was frigid, and both of us were shivering. The bleak, cold air crept in through the windows of the bus. The vehicle had no heater. We wrapped ourselves inside our blankets. I had become car sick and was vomiting frequently. Ali had gotten scared. He brought a bucket for me and kept asking how I was doing. I nodded to show I was fine. Due to the cold weather, the bus did not break at the stopover, so we ate breakfast and lunch inside the bus. I had prepared boiled egg sandwiches with pickled cucumber and tomatoes. The bus stopped for prayers, however. I stepped off the bus and opened the water tap to perform ablution; it was icy-cold. When I tried to wash my face, my whole body began to quiver. My teeth were chattering. The *mohr*[50] I used for *sajdah* (prostration) was so

---

50. *Mohr* is a formed clay or a piece of stone, on which Shias prostrate when performing prayers. According to the Shiite jurisprudence, in their prayers, Muslims must put their foreheads upon the earth whatever grows from the earth on the condition that it is non-edible and non-wearable. For this reason, Shias built

cold I could feel it through my bones. I was reciting my prayers and shivering.

In Ardabil, we first went to a motel to rest. Two or three hours later, Ali went out to call his friend. He was supposed to rent a house for us. We packed our belongings and left. The house had a shared yard and three rooms. The landlord was called Mr. Karimi, who lived in one of the rooms along with his wife and a two or three-year-old boy. The next room had been rented by a three-member family with a little girl. So, we occupied the last room. The room was cold. We used an electric heater. I used that heater for cooking, too. Sometimes I made fish, sometimes *adasi*.[51] Every time I decided to make *adasi*, I had to put the lentil on the heater the night before. As for the fish, first I had to cook the rice and fry the fish in turns. I also cooked other foods, but mostly fish and *adasi*. Living in Ardabil was hard due to the freezing air. We had grown up in Lar and had never experienced such cold

---

small soil or stone pieces, on which prostration is valid.
51. *Adasi* or *aash adas* (literally, lentil soup) is an Iranian dish, mainly made of lentils, with the addition of onion, dried mint, herbs, and fried onion slices.

weather. The water taps in the yard were frozen and had been shut off. I remember my hands became completely numb when I tried to sweep the yard. My hand froze around the broom and took its shape. I held my hand in front of the heater so that it could recover to its normal form after a while. When I hung the laundry out to dry, it would also freeze. I collected and put them in front of the heater arduously. Even when we were in Lar, I always washed the clothes by hand. I had a washing machine in my dowry, but I loved to wash Ali's clothes with my own hands. Once I felt severe pain in my hands after washing clothes with cold water. Ali became very upset when he found out. I went out of my way for Ali and said, "I'd love to wash Abu al-Fazl's clothes with my own hands." I used to iron his clothes. I always folded his left sleeve carefully and attentively and then ironed it. I never let it become puckered. I made the shirt ready for him to be worn without any discomfort.

It was a long way to the university. Ali went out early in the morning and came back in the evening. He could have stayed in the university's dormitory if it wasn't for me. But he turned a blind eye to all the difficulties for my sake. I did not miss my family and city during those thirty days in Ardabil. Ali and I were separated for so long that I had given my heart only to him during this time, and I could think of no one and nothing else. I was trying to compensate for all those gloomy days. Ali used to burn the midnight oil to study. I also stayed awake with him to rewrite the handouts he had taken from his friends. "You should go to bed," he said. "No, I came here to be with you, not for sleeping. I would have stayed in Lar, otherwise," I said. Sometimes, we stayed up until three in the morning. Ali studied, and I wrote the handouts.

One night, he said, "Let's go to the public telephone center tomorrow and call our families." We had no landlines at home. On the way there, I looked around the city; it was strange. There was snow on every corner. Salt had been distributed on the sidewalks. In Lar, it never snowed, but in Ardabil, there was nothing but snow everywhere. Talking to my mother-in-law, "Mom! Give us your sun; we will give you our snow in return!" I said.

I used to recite the Quran when I was alone. Also, sometimes I played with Mrs. Karimi's little boy. He was chubby and cute, around two years and a few months of age; however, he looked four or five. Mrs. Karimi entrusted her baby to me when she was going to school. There was always tea brewing on their heater. They used to drink thyme tea in addition to black tea. She said, "We end up drinking too much black tea and sugar due to the intense cold; we get tired of them. So we turn to other plants, herbal tea, dried mulberries, and raisins." I took her baby to my house to play with. I loved babies, especially that adorable one. He was fair-skinned with red cheeks. I troubled him and said, "You are naughty," and to me he replied, "You are naughty, too."

During the last days in Ardabil, we went shopping. I liked their brooms. Contrary to the brooms in our city, they weren't made of palm leaves. They were made of millet stalks. I bought a few brooms that day. When we returned to Lar, my sister-in-law fancied brooms, so I gave her one of them.

It seemed I was doomed to always remain expectant for Ali. Back in Lar, Ali went to the frontline, and I went to stay with my mother-in-law again. I cannot recall now why I went into one of the rooms. Suddenly, a creature walking on the wall with a curled tail caught my sight. I became so excited, shouting, "Come and take a glance at God's blessing! It's so pretty!" My brother-in-law came in. When he saw the scorpion that got me so excited, he said, "Who are you?! This is a scorpion! Aren't you scared of scorpions?!" I replied, "Why should I be scared of it?" I had heard a lot about scorpions, but I had never seen one from up close before. It was so pretty. All of Ali's family members knew that I was so fearless. Now, this incident had given them the proof. My brother-in-law explained the story to Ali in detail when he came back from the frontline. Ali burst out laughing.

Chapter 5

The Official Officer

In February 1987, Ali was formally recruited as a guardian by the IRGC. Mr. Ayatollahi gifted Ali the IRGC's uniform in the Friday Prayer. I forced him to try it on instantly when he came home, though he did not want to wear it right at that moment. He went and put the uniform on. I was as overjoyed as if God had given me the entire world. I was proud that I was the wife of a *pasdar*.[52]

He was with me for fifteen days and fifteen days at the frontline from that day

---

52. *Pāsdār* (literally, guard) is a person who serves in the Islamic Revolutionary Guard Corps, who has the duty of guarding and protecting the values of the Islamic Revolution.

forward. His mood and actions changed more each time he returned from the frontline. All of what he did and what he said smelled like a testament. He followed the backlog of the delayed works in order to finish them. One of them was related to the land on which we had built our house. The land belonged to Ali's uncle, who lived in Dubai. Ali said he had to visit his uncle to speak with him about the land. He was at unrest and said, "I have to take his full consent." His uncle had already bestowed us the land, yet Ali was still doubtful. He backpacked and traveled to Dubai for a few days. I do not know what his uncle told him. I never asked about these things. I even had no idea how much Ali's salary was. Upon return, his uncle had sent me a precious necklace. Ali had also brought me a brown-colored flounce shirt and a *chador* as a souvenir. I tried on the shirt as soon as he gave it to me. It was ill-fitting, too baggy, and long in sleeves and height. I intended to shorten it, but I could not find it in my heart to do it. "You don't tamper with a gift," I said. I wore it as it was in front of him.

When he was not home, I tried to entertain myself so that I would be less plagued by negative thoughts. But it was away itself," I said. "Stop it. You have to visit a doctor," he said. He could not come with me, so he called Mr. Khalil Azad, who lived near the hospital. Ali asked him to send his wife with me to the hospital. I went with Farahnaz. The doctor examined my hand and said, "It's because of anxiety. Ma'am! What's the cause of your anxiety?" I did not say anything.

Could anyone understand me? Could anyone understand that when your husband goes to the frontline, it's 'operation time' day and night in your heart, and you die a thousand deaths? Could anyone understand how every doorbell ring sets your soul on fire when your husband is not home? Could anyone understand what you are going through when, in your best days of youth, instead of hearing about hope for the future, you constantly hear about death?

He talked a lot about his martyrdom. He was making his will the entire time: "You have to continue your studies if I am martyred; take care of my family, etc." It was too much for me to bear. I said, "Who says you will die first? Maybe I'll die first." It made me cry. I said, "Ali, you have to not possible. I ruminated about him every second. Is he going to be safe? What if a shootout takes him from me? I sat on the prayer rug and tried to relieve myself from my sorrow by praying and reciting the Quran. These worries were for a reason, it turned out. When he came back home on leave, I figured out from his crumbled face that his big toe was bothering him again. A PRC 77[53] had once fallen on his big toe in the frontline during our engagement period. After that, a second nail grew beneath his nail and hurt him every now and then. He said, "Tooba! Hold on to my toe firmly. Don't look at my face, so you don't let it go!" I grabbed his toe very firmly. He pulled out the second nail with a nail clipper. It hurt him a lot. He would bite his knee so no one could hear his yells.

Day by day, my moods were changing, too. I feared I may lose Ali. I was restless and expressed my sadness more than before. Until then, I only cried in privacy, but now, I even cried in front of him. I cried when washing the dishes. I cried when cooking.

---

53. AN/PRC 77 Radio Set is a heavy manpack system used during the imposed war.

Ali said nothing and only looked at me kindly. His looks reduced me to tears even more. I said, "I'm sorry. I'm not to blame. I can't stand it. I can't help crying."

> *The man was saying his prayers in the middle of the night. The woman was looking at him from far off. She would watch him as he recited his prayers. It was a pleasant scene for her. He had lost one of his hands for God, and now, he said takbir,[54] performed ruku[55] and sajdah with his remaining hand. Ali said his prayers, and Tooba tried to calm herself down. Ali talked to God and Tooba to her heart. Finishing with his prayers, Tooba sat beside him. They recited the Quran together. It was their morning routine.*

I wept and wailed so much that I started to feel severe pain in my hand. I screamed from pain every time I moved. Ali insisted that I had to visit a doctor. "The pain will go

---

54. "*Allahu akbar*" means that God is greater. This is one of the most sacred *dhikr* or mottos recited by Muslims, which is part of the daily prayer.
55. *Ruku* is an action in the prayer. It is to bend until the fingers of one's hands reach the knee.

perform my *ghusl* of the dead,[56] It is I that will submit my will to you." I only said these words to comfort myself.

I felt like having a baby, a keepsake from Ali that I could keep after his departure. Someone I could look to for comfort, "If God took Ali from me, at least I have a child from him," I prayed. "No, Tooba! Don't pray to God for a child. I begged God not to give us a child. I don't want you to be troubled after me. You could live more comfortably without a baby." Ali said. It broke my heart. How could I live more comfortably without Ali? Could I even live without him?!

Winter turned into spring. It was the turn of the year. New Year's holidays arrived in a home where I was alone. Ali was at the frontline. When I was feeling down, I went from my mother-in-law's house to ours under the guise of dusting. I stared at the walls and reviewed all of my memories. I took his clothes out of the closet and folded them again. I laid out his prayer mat. I said prayers and recited the Quran or looked at

---

56. *Ghusl mass al-mayyit* is a ritual bath obligatory upon theone who has touched the dead body after it has cooled.

our wedding photos. Ali had brought rifle bullet casings and a deactivated shell. I had put them in the niche. Now that he was not here, I took more time cleaning them and putting them back in place.

Ali had missed me too, it seemed. He sent us a letter—to me as well as his family. He had written the whole text on a single piece of paper. My father-in-law, who knew what I was going through, said, "Tooba! You read first."

She ran into the room, closed her eyes, and held the letter close to her heart. She had missed the writer of the letter so much. She took a few big, deep breaths and opened her eyes. She kissed the letter and started to read; tears kept falling from her eyes. Suddenly, she felt a lump in her throat. Grief and sadness engulfed her. She stood up fiercely, took a pen, and scribbled on the letter. "…I beg you to remarry after I am martyred…". When she was done, she threw it away. She put her head on her knees and broke down into tears. She understood that everything was coming to an end. Her life with Ali was evaporating. She felt like someone had held her throat firmly. She was choking. She cried her heart out

completely. When she gave the letter to her father-in-law, her eyes were still full of tears.

My father-in-law took the letter, and the scribbled part caught his eyes. When Ali returned, he asked him, "What have you written on this part that…." Ali held his head down and said, "Aghajoon maybe she preferred that you should not know about it." I felt like complaining, but I buttoned up. I kept it in my heart. "*He's tired. These words bother him more,*" I thought to myself. "*If I tell him I can't stand his words, I may prevent him from achieving his dream. He may be unable to part ways with me,*" I also thought. But Ali had already parted ways with me. During the last few days, I understood him.

On the morning of March 31, he came back to Lar. Mr. Eslampanah invited us for dinner, and we decided to go to the desert the next day. We slept in their house at night to set off from there in the morning. They laid out a carpet on one side for the women and another on the other side for the men. The men started to play soccer in between the two carpets. I was staring at Ali. He was very good at soccer. He had red sweatpants on and was running around. I was very anxious. I was usually jolted awake by the nightmare that Ali had been martyred. Ali asked me to help him perform ablution. I became more worried and anxious. Maybe it is better to say I was frightened. Typically, he would not request such things. I felt that he was looking at me strangely. Again, I tried to convince myself that these were just delusions.

Chapter 6

Take Me to Lady Zahra (s) on Your Wings

We spent the *sizdah be-dar* day there and returned home. Ali went to the IRGC base as soon as he arrived. He was going to go back to the frontline on the same day after *maghrib* and *isha* prayers. I laid out his prayer rug, and he performed his prayers. He said his *takbir* out loud, *'Allahu akbar.'* My heart trembled inside me. It felt like the ground beneath my feet also shook. He performed the *ruku*, *sajdah*, etc. I had leaned against the niche on which we had settled the casings and mortar shell. While gazing fixedly at Ali, tears were flowing from my eyes. I had found out that he would never come back this time. When he said the *salam*[57] of his prayers, I sat beside him and held his hand. I said, "It is said that in the Battle of Mu'tah,[58] Ja'far al-Tayyār[59] lost both of his hands, and in return, God granted him two wings in heaven. So God will definitely bless you with a wing too. I beg you to give me a ride on your wing and take me to visit Fatimah al-Zahra (S), okay?" My tears rolled down from the corner of my eyes onto our hands. Ali said nothing and performed *sajdah*. He stood up. The lump in my throat was choking me. I had a lot in my heart. Then, I carried myself and said, "Do you remember the day you proposed to me? You asked if I could bear it if you became disabled, POW (prisoner of war), or martyred. Did I not bear it, Ali?" He said nothing and only

---

57. *Salam* is the final part of the *Salat* in Islam after *tashahhud*.

58. The Battle of Mu'tah was a war between the Islamic army of Prophet Muhammad (s) and the Roman army, which took place in 8 AH (629 CE) in the Mu'tah area at the border of Levant.

59. Ja'far b. Abi Talib (martyrdom 629 AH), known as Ja'far al-Tayyar, was the Prophet's (s) cousin and an older brother of Imam 'Ali (a). He was greatly honored by the Prophet (s). Ja'far was martyred in the Battle of Mu'ta. His mausoleum is located in Jordan.

nodded as a yes. I do not know. Maybe Ali was also choking, just like me. "I'll bear it if you're martyred, too. Ali, tell me anything you would like to tell people. I will deliver a speech at your funeral," I continued. He said everything he wanted, and I wrote everything down. He recited his *isha* prayers. I went and fetched the Quran, as well as a glass of water. I fastened his dog tag myself. I held the Quran above his head,[60] myself. Ali kissed the Quran and passed from underneath it. I closed the door and burst into tears. I was sobbing uncontrollably in the room. So much crying made my eyes heavy-lidded, and I drifted off to sleep. At midnight, I opened my eyes slightly and saw Ali sitting by, gazing at me! He never used to wake me up. He usually shook me gently so that I woke up. But that night, he had not even done that. I smiled. "What are you doing here!?" I asked. "I couldn't go. We

---

60. Holding the Quran on the head is a ritual whereby Shias ask God to forgive their sins by making resort to the Quran, the Prophet (s), Lady Fatima al-Zahra (a), and the Twelve Imams (a). The ritual is conveyed from Shiite Imams in Shiite books of supplication. It is performed on Nights of *Qadr* in the month of Ramadan.

went to Evaz,[61] and then I came back. I told others I'll make it myself tomorrow. Tooba! These last few days, we have been busy with too many parties; we didn't get the chance to talk to each other," he said.

The last night of our marriage was beautiful. We talked so much that night to compensate for the days and nights we were not together. When the *adhan* was recited, Ali performed his prayers and left.

Thursday that same week, we were informed that Ali was injured. My mother-in-law's house became crowded. All of the relatives came over. I knew everything. I knew that Ali had become martyred, and they were not telling me to keep me calm. The men knew it, but they had not broken the news to the women, so that they would not reveal it. One of my mother's neighbors had come over to comfort me. She told me that Ali had only been injured and that I should not be worried. I leaned and whispered, "Masoumeh! Ali has been martyred." She asked, "How do you know!?" I said, "I dreamt about it." They tried to

---

61. Evaz is a city and capital of Evaz County, in Fars Province, Iran.

cover up the story until after *maghrib* and *isha* prayers. After the prayers, Hamzeh, Ali's brother-in-law, came to me. He, too, said that my Ali has been wounded. I replied, "My husband has been martyred. This is the key to our house. Please go fetch his picture frame from the niche for the funeral." He just stared at me, stunned, saying nothing. He went and told Haj Abbas, "We thought she didn't know anything! But she knew everything!" Now, everyone could speak freely about Ali's martyrdom.

They brought Ali's body on the fifteenth of Sha'ban.[62] I do not know the coincidence, but Ali was born in the month of Sha'ban, injured in the month of Sha'ban, and martyred in the same month as well. There were also two other martyrs in addition to Ali, shaheed Najaf Ali Mofid, who had made every effort for our city, and shaheed Muhammad Ali Farasat. Shaheed Farasat was his family's only child. He was a *Qari* (professional reciter) of the Quran and a life skills teacher. That night was supposed to be

---

62. Mid-Sha'ban (Sha'ban 15th) is the birthday of Imam al-Mahdi (a), the Twelfth Shiite Imam, whom Shias believe to be the promised savior.

his wedding night. He had told his mother, "I'll catch up for the Mid-Sha'ban night." He managed to catch up to that very night, not for the wedding, but for the funeral, indeed.

It was a crowded funeral. People had also come from nearby villages. Before our marriage, Ali regularly went to these villages for plumbing and masonry work. He carried the materials to the villages for the job and never took even a single rial from anyone. They all had come to pray for Ali. They dispersed the crowd and asked the martyrs' families to come to see the bodies. I gently drifted forward and sat beside him. My aunts sat next to me and looked after me. I drew the shroud away. I suddenly became sickened. Ali had been burnt. No eyelashes, no beard, no hair. I could barely breathe. I wiped my tears away using the corner of my chador. My hands were trembling. I whispered, "Peace be upon you, O Aba Abdullah, and on the souls who died with you..."[63] A deep sense of grief overtook me. Every sorrow in

---

63. Part of Ziyarat Ashura (Supplication of Ashura). A very prevalent supplication often recited on the day of Ashura by Shia Muslims.

the world was bursting into my heart. It is very hard when you cannot pour your heart out and calm down! I was about to scream out, but I had to keep silent. Not only was I not feeling well myself, but also, my mother was admitted to the hospital after learning of Ali's martyrdom. On the day of the funeral, neither my mom nor *Aghajaan* were present at the ceremony—only my siblings. We looked at each other and broke into tears. My legs were numb. I went through the crowd toward Mr. Me'marzadeh, who was eulogizing on the microphone. From the beginning of the Islamic Revolution, Mr. Me'marzadeh chanted slogans on every occasion with a microphone. I asked him to hand me the microphone so that I could read the will of the shaheed to the crowd.

> *She took the microphone; her hands were trembling. Her whole body was shivering. She stared at Ali's coffin. She couldn't see anyone except him. "In the name of Allah. I am the wife of shaheed Sha'ban Ali Afifeh, and I'm going to read his will to you. To all the women who are like my sisters, I advise you to observe your hijab because your hijab is sharper than our sword and redder than our blood. To all the men who are like*

> *my brothers! I beg you to stand behind Imam Khomeini until the war is going on and don't let the war end up for the benefit of the Ba'athists."[64] The sound of people mourning filled her ears; her eyes were wet. Blurred was the scene of Ali's coffin. Her teardrops fell on her cheeks as she closed her eyes, drew her chador on her face, gave the microphone back, and went away.*

People stood in lines. Mr. Ayatollahi recited prayers for the blessings of the martyrs. With each *takbir* he said, it brought our wedding day back into my mind. "Ms. Tooba Mo'tamed! Will you take him as your husband? For the second time, will you? For the third time…." I could not stand hearing Mr. Ayatollahi's voice playing on the speakers. I wished I was deaf and heard nothing. I wished I was buried along with Ali. When they were throwing soil on Ali, I told him, "I'm coming, whether today or tomorrow; you know I can't tolerate it."

---

64. Ba'athis are members and supporters of the Iraqi Arab Socialist Ba'ath party, which seized power in Iraq in the final decades of the twentieth century.. The Iraqi war on Iran occurred during the reign of this party.

I was out of sorts for a couple of weeks. When I stood to perform my prayers, I broke down into tears. I had no control over myself. Memories haunted me constantly. Ali's fellow combatants told me how he was martyred. The vehicle Ali had been riding was full of ammunition. It was a loot they were taking to the rear. The mortar shell fell right on the vehicle, and the ammos blasted off. Some became martyred in that incident, and some were thrown out of the vehicle. Ali had been completely burnt. Those who survived were also very sick. When I pictured these scenes, I could not eat anything. My aunts and relatives would bring us food, but I abstained from it. They forced me to eat at least one date. However, I did not enjoy eating that either. It turned into a lump in my throat. Everything happened and ended so fast that I still could not believe it.

Sometimes I felt Ali would come back, like the previous times. But the black shirt I had on made me remember everything. Missing Ali was like a heap of sorrow in my heart. My eyes were always wet. My friends and relatives came by to offer me condolences. One of my friends said, "Tooba! Ali is no longer alive, but you are. You have to keep on living. Will your tears make him come back?" Although these words were burdensome, they helped me get a grip.

A few months after Ali was martyred, I heard on TV that Azad Islamic University enrolls students without a diploma degree requirement. I followed it up and bought the books I had to read. I read books and studied constantly. I thought to myself, "Ali would be pleased that I'm continuing my studies, and he is seeing me now." These words inspired me. I passed the entrance exam. Once, the university's president came into our class and asked, "Who has passed the exam without a diploma?" I raised my hand. He smiled and said, "Ma'am, you are the only one who's been accepted without a diploma in the whole country. I think this circular has been approved only for you!" His words were full of hope for me. I felt like God has blessed me greatly, and Ali has not left me alone. I studied hard and went to the *hawza* as well. I became a teacher after a while, something I aspired to become from childhood. After a few years, I went to Qom along with my brother, who was a seminary scholar, to live in the neighborhood of

Fatimah al-Masumah (s)[65]. I served in the shoe-keeping room of Fatimah al-Masumah's shrine for sixteen years. It was a place I could be at peace. Even now, I keep my sorrows from Ali's absence in my heart, to pour them out to Fatimah al-Masumah (S) when I go there. I beg her to pray to God for me to be with Ali. I really do not know when my prayers will be answered.

---

65. Fatimah al-Ma'sumah (d. 816), known as Lady Ma'sumah, was the daughter of Imam al-Kazim (a) and the sister of Imam al-Ridha (a). Lady Ma'sumah moved from Medina towards Khorasan in 816 at the request of her brother Imam al-Ridha (a). However, she was stricken with illness on her journey. For this reason, she went to Qom, where she stayed in the house of Musa b. Khazraj al-Ash'ari. After seventeen days of her stay in Qom, she passed away, and her body was buried in that city.

www.ingramcontent.com/pod-product-compliance
Lightning Source LLC
Chambersburg PA
CBHW030041100526
44590CB00011B/294